On Christmas Eve

written by **Judy Zocchi**

illustrated by **Rebecca Wallis**

dingles&company New Jersey

First printing

PUBLISHED BY dingles&company
P.O. Box 508 • Sea Girt, New Jersey • 08750
WEBSITE: www.dingles.com • E-MAIL: info@dingles.com

Library of Congress Catalog Card No.: 2004091568
ISBN: 1-891997-47-5

Printed in the United States of America

For Mom who always made sure the piles were even.

ART DIRECTION & DESIGN Barbie Lambert
ENGLISH EDITED BY Andrea Curley
RESEARCH AND ADDITIONAL COPY WRITTEN BY Robert Neal Kanner
EDUCATIONAL CONSULTANT Anita Tarquinio-Marcocci
DESIGN ASSISTANT Erin Collity
CRAFT PHOTOGRAPHY BY Sara Sagliano
CRAFT CREATED BY the Aldorasi family
PRE-PRESS BY Pixel Graphics

Holiday Happenings

examines the
most popular holidays
celebrated by various cultures.
The series explains
the origin of each day
as well as popular traditions
and activities
associated with it.

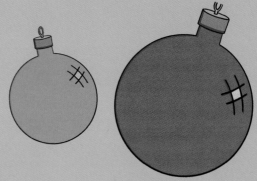

On Christmas Eve
you might decorate
your Christmas tree

The custom of decorating
evergreen trees at Christmastime
began in Germany. Trees were decorated
with apples and candles. Later the
custom traveled to England
and then to America.

with candy canes and glass balls.

Then **you**
go caroling
and **sing**
"Deck the Halls."

On Christmas Eve
you could wrap a present

Red and green are the traditional colors of Christmas. For Christians, red symbolizes the blood of Jesus, which was shed at his death, and green represents both life continuing through the winter and eternal life.

with paper that's red or green.

Then you put it in a stocking so it will not be seen.

On Christmas Eve
you might see A statue
in a manger

At Christmastime, some
families re-create the birthplace
of Jesus in their homes. They set up a scene
that includes statues of the baby Jesus lying
in a manger, his mother, Mary,
and his earthly father, Joseph.

Gabriel is said to be the angel who blows a horn before making announcements. He is the angel who told Mary that she would give birth to Jesus, the Son of God.

and an angel blowing a horn.

Then you celebrate the day that Jesus was born.

At Christmastime, families all over the world prepare holiday foods together. Baking sugar cookies shaped like Christmas trees, candy canes, and other Christmas decorations is a popular tradition in America.

On Christmas Eve
you might bake cookies

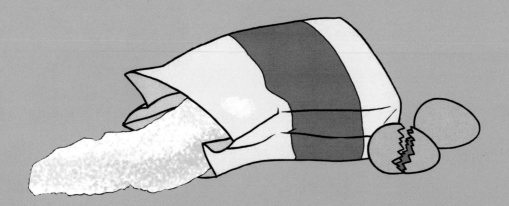

and leave them on a table or shelf.

It is an old American tradition
to leave milk and cookies as a snack for
Santa on Christmas Eve.

While you're sleeping, they might be eaten by Santa Claus himself.

Christmas

Christmas is the holiday that celebrates the birth of Jesus Christ. Christians believe an angel told Mary that she would bear Jesus, the Son of God. Just before Jesus was due to be born, Mary and her husband, Joseph, had to  go to Bethlehem. When they got there, they could not find any place to stay except a stable. That was where Jesus was born. His cradle was a hay-filled manger. The word "Christmas" comes from the old English word "Cristes masses", or Christ's Mass. American Christmas traditions are a combination of German, Dutch, and English customs. From Germany came the tradition of decorating Christmas trees with glass ornaments. The Dutch shared their Santa Claus legends. The English brought many traditions, including burning a large log called the Yule log. Christmas is celebrated on December 25.

DID YOU KNOW...

Use the Holiday Happenings series to expose children to the world around them.

- In 1836, Alabama was the first state to recognize Christmas as an official holiday. Oklahoma was the last state, proclaiming Christmas a legal holiday in 1907.
- In the Ukraine, Christmas trees often have an artificial spider and web as decorations because finding a spiderweb on Christmas morning is considered to bring good luck!
- Every time a Christmas tree is harvested, two or three seedlings are planted in its place.
- More than three billion Christmas cards are sent annually in the United States alone.
- Towns in the United States that have Christmas-themed names include Santa Claus, Arizona; Santa Claus, Indiana; Noel, Missouri; Christmas, Arizona; and Christmas, Florida.

BUILDING CHARACTER...

Use the Holiday Happenings series to help instill positive character traits in children. This Christmas emphasize Generosity.

- What does it mean to be generous?
- To whom can we be generous?
- Do you have to buy and give big presents to be generous?
- What can you do to show generosity to someone in your community?

CULTURE CONNECTION...

Use the Holiday Happenings series to expand children's view of other cultures.

- Find out which countries celebrate Christmas.
- How do they celebrate Christmas?
- Are these celebrations similar to the way you celebrate Christmas?

TRY SOMETHING NEW...

Save your extra change every night for a month before Christmas and then use it to buy a toy for a needy child.

For more information on the Holiday Happenings series or to find activities that coordinate with it, explore our website at **www.dingles.com**.

Christmas Gift Tags

Goal: To create gift tags using recycled Christmas cards

Craft: Christmas gift tags

Materials:

recycled Christmas cards, red- and green-colored ribbons, ruler, hole puncher, pinking shears, colored marker

Directions:

1. Gather materials.

2. Turn the Christmas cards face up so you can see all of the pictures on them.

3. Choose the Christmas card pictures you would like to use for your gift tags. Use pinking shears to cut out the pictures. (You can make your tags as big or as small as you like.)

4. Once you have cut out the pictures, use the hole puncher to make a hole in the upper left-hand corner or in the top center of each tag.

5. Cut the ribbon into pieces that are at least 9 inches long.

6. Push a piece of ribbon through each hole and tie a knot, making a loop that you will use to tape your tag onto a gift.

7. Turn over each tag. Using the colored marker, write the words "To" and "From" on each tag.

8. Now you are ready to address your tags and attach them to gifts!

Judy Zocchi

is the author of the Global Adventures, Holiday Happenings, Click & Squeak's Computer Basics, and Paulie and Sasha series. She is a writer and lyricist who holds a bachelor's degree in fine arts/theater from Mount Saint Mary's College and a master's degree in educational theater from New York University. She lives in Manasquan, New Jersey, with her husband, David.

Rebecca Wallis

was born in Cornwall, England, and has a bachelor's degree in illustration from Falmouth College of Arts. She has illustrated a wide variety of books for children, and she divides her time between Cornwall and London.